# THE SOHO LEOPARD

Ruth Padel has published five collections of poetry, most recently *Voodoo Shop*, shortlisted for the Whitbread and T.S. Eliot Prizes. Her *52 Ways of Looking at a Poem* is a sparkling introduction to contemporary poetry in Britain. A regular contributor to BBC Radio 4's *Saturday Review*, she is a Fellow of the Royal Society of Literature, and also of the Zoological Society of London.

www.ruthpadel.com

# THE SOHO LEOPARD

Ruth Padel

Chatto & Windus
LONDON

Published by Chatto & Windus 2004

2 4 6 8 10 9 7 5 3 1

Copyright © Ruth Padel 2004

Ruth Padel has asserted her right under the Copyright, Designs
and Patents Act 1988 to be identified as the author of this work

First published in Great Britain in 2004 by
Chatto & Windus
Random House, 20 Vauxhall Bridge Road,
London SW1V 2SA

Random House Australia (Pty) Limited
20 Alfred Street, Milsons Point, Sydney,
New South Wales 2061, Australia

Random House New Zealand Limited
18 Poland Road, Glenfield,
Auckland 10, New Zealand

Random House (Pty) Limited
Endulini, 5A Jubilee Road, Parktown 2193, South Africa

The Random House Group Limited Reg. No. 954009
www.randomhouse.co.uk

A CIP catalogue record for this book
is available from the British Library

ISBN 0 7011 7621 0

Papers used by Random House are natural,
recyclable products made from wood grown in sustainable forests;
the manufacturing processes conform to the environmental
regulations of the country of origin

Typeset by Deltatype Ltd, Birkenhead, Merseyside

Printed and bound in Great Britain by
Mackays of Chatham plc

For Kerin Hope

Μὰ τί γυρεύουν οἱ ψυχές μας ταξιδεύοντας

# ACKNOWLEDGEMENTS

Thanks to the editors of: *Boomerang* (www.boomeranguk.com), *Discourses: Poems for the Royal Institution* (ed. J. Shapcott and S. Ede), Royal Institution in association with Calouste Gulbenkian Foundation, 2002); *London Magazine; London Review of Books; Melic Review; New Writing 11* (ed. A. O'Hagan and C. Tóibin, Picador, 2002); *Poetry International Festival Brochure 2002*; *Poetry London; Poetry Proms 2002* (BBC Publications). Also to the editors of the Crocodile Specialist Group website.

'The King's Cross Foxes' was commissioned by Artangel for Richard Wentworth's exhibition on King's Cross, *An Area of Outstanding Unnatural Beauty.* 'Mary's Elephant, Elizabeth's Spinet' was commissioned by the Poetry Book Society and the Victoria and Albert Museum. Thanks for commissions to Jo Shapcott and Colm Tóibin, Julia Bird of the Poetry Book Society, Siân Ede of the Calouste Gulbenkian Foundation, James Lingwood of Artangel, Fiona McClean of the BBC. And to Stephen Harris of Bristol University for advice on urban foxes.

Thanks also to the Author's Foundation for help in buying time to write, through an award administered by the Society of Authors; to the British Council for sending me to do readings and workshops in Myanmar; and to the Calouste Gulbenkian Foundation for funds from their 'Arts and Science' programme towards research in Karnataka, South India, shared with Dr Ullas Karanth of the Wildlife Conservation Society.

Many thanks, with love, to Elaine, Jo and Neil for criticism and comment, and to my Chatto editor, Rebecca Carter, for her care, patience and judgement as well as her comments. Warm thanks and love also to my outside editor Christopher Reid.

*Caution. There are alligators in areas of these Gardens. Under no circumstances should you feed or approach them. They are wild animals and should be treated with great care.*

Entrance card to the Jungle Gardens of Avery Island, Louisiana

# CONTENTS

## IV   NIGHTS OF THE DRY MONSOON

# TIGER DRINKING AT FOREST POOL

Water, moonlight, danger, dream.
  Bronze urn, angled on a tree-root: one
  Slash of light, then gone. A red moon
Seen through clouds, or almost seen.

Treasure found but lost, flirting between
  The worlds of lost and found. An unjust law
  Repealed, a wish come true, a lifelong
Sadness healed. Haven, in the mind,

To anyone hurt by littleness. A prayer,
  For the moment, saved; treachery forgiven.
  Flame of the crackle-glaze tangle, amber
Reflected in grey milk-jade. An old song
  Remembered, long debt paid.
  A painting on silk, which may fade.

# I

## THE TANGLED BANK

*It is interesting to contemplate an entangled bank, clothed with many plants of many kinds, with birds singing on the bushes, with various insects flitting about, and with worms crawling through the damp earth, and to reflect that these elaborately constructed forms, so different from each other, and dependent upon each other in so complex a manner, have all been produced by laws acting around us . . .*

*There is grandeur in this view of life, with its several powers, having been originally breathed into a few forms or into one; and that, whilst this planet has gone on cycling according to the fixed law of gravity, from so simple a beginning endless forms most beautiful and most wonderful have been, and are being, evolved.*

Charles Darwin, *On the Origin of Species*

# MARY'S ELEPHANT, ELIZABETH'S SPINET

Some night in the 1580s, she snaps the last knot off with her
                                                         teeth
By candle-light. One blob under the tail and she has him, in tent
Stitch: startled king from *Icones Animalium*, a beast she's never
                                                          seen.
Ears, silver-pink abalone. Feet lost in a webbed pool
Of bubbles: blue muttonfat peas. She rests him on her lap
Writing letters in her head, unsendable as words for resin
In Armenian akrolect. Her cousin knows everything she has to
                                                           say
Already. It's been said. Outside, the black unbroken forest
Rides to London. Wolves kill a roe, for cubs whose last
                                                    descendent
Will be shot in Mary's realm, two hundred years down the line.
But she, in these walls, is marigold: a heliotrope,
Turning to sun that'll never warm her skin again,
Ransacking old books in Spanish for emblems of hope.

Down south, the keyboard's come from Florian, in Venice.
Cousin E tries some Byrdian version of *Only the Lonely,* checks
The gilt inlay, Islamic painted whorls, the logo of falcon and
                                                        sceptre.
(Her mum's. She paid extra for that.) This sound-hole; a fretted
Bronze rose, is an eavesdropping sun. She's awaiting her
                                                        spies.
She can never give in. She has become her own grotesque:
She sends men to the tropics, men to death. When her blood
                                                         says
Dance, she will gavotte the night away with the Earl of
                                                    Leicester.
Are there tears at what she looks like now, for who on earth else
May show up in her bed? When melancholy strikes, they see
Her turn to a Pavane. Shadow-bones, capitate, triquetral, lunate,
Stripe and flinch in the back of her hand. One frizzed hair,
White and red, drifts down over black middle C.

And if you and I held hands across this room, touched DNA
Of *their* touch sloughed off on this tusker
Embroidered in velvet and lint, this Venice lacquer,
Cypress, ebony, we would join fingerprints that never met.

# THE RED-GOLD BORDER

*If an eye wants to know itself,* he said,
*it looks into the thing most like it in the world:*
*another eye. Closed-bracket lovers,*
*watching their own flame flicker*
*in a burnished pick-up mirror of each other.*

Though Plato doesn't add it, let's pretend
Socrates sighed then; leaned against the glow
of Alcibiades in shadow, loose
red-gold-bordered tunic opening to show
bronze thighs (and look, one knee up) splayed

on the cushioned bench, little duck-tail rivulets
of sweat-curled dark hair feathering
those famous soldier's muscles. Close, too close, beside
the snub-nosed simian recusenik
chopping logic in the sweet-oil light

as Samian wine went round the board
and flute-girls danced in panther-spotted chitons.
Yes; his golden boy, out always to seduce,
who'd grow up to destroy
the white imperial city he adored.

# JAGUAR QUARTET

## I  SAVIOUR

Listen to Itzamna, King of the Mayan sky,
the God-Who's-Entirely-Good. 'Jaguar Sun,'
he says, 'springs new each day in a bubble of fire
where the Children of Hacauitz,
God of the Silent Mountain, sleep in the east.

Jaguar runs through the sky all day
on his Lucozade paws. Twelve hours he burns,
tattooing the blue with peyote rosettes
from his ormolu skin, till he dives to the west
where he wrestles all night

with the blood-heavy Lords of Xibalba.
(The shadow-clot Underworld, brother.
Name it, and shudder.) Jaguar's power
is warding off. To keep evil out of your home,
yourself, your village, build him a shrine

at each possible exit. Kill him a rosy agouti.
Weave him a spirit house from chalice vine.
Hang it from adobe cactus, stud it
with Purple Queen Cajeput, Lucky Nut,
Green Belly Mushroom, all the atropines,

narcotics, phytotoxins, glycosides
from our home store of poisonous plants.
The secret of apotropaic
is fighting a danger with danger.
One single seed can prove fatal.'

## 2  THE HAND THAT FED HIM

Yaguara, Beast-That-Kills-in-One-Bound,
with his flaring nostrils, pointed teeth,
his black and gold. God of the Amazon
Over-Lord of Fire. Men scrambled with bare hands

to bag a peccary or capybara, gob it raw.
Jaguar had arrows, forty kinds of bow.
Jaguar dined on chops, black juices, *flambés*,
roast. But Masters, hear the moral.

Jaguar was generous. He took pity: brought home
a hungry hunter, taught him crossbow, longbow, pipe.
In Jaguar's cave for the first time Man saw flame.
Saw yellow-red in dark. Saw smoke. Saw biting flies

stop biting, rainforest draw back its damp
from a paling skirt of mud. Grilled crocodile?
Broiled anteater? Fab! So new, so now.
Went down a treat, not even touching the sides.

You're everything I've ever loved,
said Man that night. But Man got up
one morning, stole the armoury, stole fire.
Men are afraid of Jaguar today,

the way you are
with someone you betrayed. You tell
yourself you had to, it's OK, don't want to see
yourself as bad; but keep away.

Now Jaguar lives alone in jungle, trying a fall
with the odd anaconda, killing his prey in a single bite.
Not the neck, you understand, but clean
through the temporal bones of the skull.

## 3 SURFACES

Chile, Paraguay, Ecuador, Brazil,
Jaguar's no longer Lord of Fire
but you trace the memoir

of something like it in his eye.
Spread Jaguar's skin
(you have to kill him first) and you unwind

a conga of orange-melt
folding and blurring through tar
like the soft-soot open-mouth kiss of pulsing gills

round an all-black coral-reef fan fish.
You're spreading the heavens in full
ceremonial dress on a starry night.


## 4 YELLOW GOURDS WITH JAGUAR IN DULWICH PIZZA HUT

Hang on a minute, soldier. No more of your party talk
or flashing the glitter lining to your fake Armani suit.
You're not the guy you were. You've no idea
how revenant you sound. As if, at Sky-Shutting-In Time

on the Rio Negro dunes, I found your stallion
thudding from the Forest-of-No-Horizon
to Place-Where-Two-Rivers-Meet, with blood
on his empty saddle. The crossbow you unsnapped, new

from its box in my kitchen, oozing each tricksy part
from the others' grooves, and tried to string,
lodging the tip in gaps between our tiles,
is slapping from the cantle, scaring him;

and its plastic handle, just the acne'd yellow-red
of crystalline isatin (precipitated
by oxidising indigo to fake-mediaeval sheen),
is cracked to its teflon heart.

So I'm on the shore with a blown horse on my hands
and you're dead as the London sandstorm
of the oolithic Age, the woolly rhinoceros
brought down by arrowheads in what will become

the Lake District, or the hippo drowned
in Thames Ditton Basin mud. And you're cold, too;
cold as the shirts – Kenzo, Versace,
Agnès B – you left on the line all night

through Brothers-Would-Not-Know-Each-Other Time.
Seventeen deep-frozen xeroxes of you
in lime-green, sky-blue, rust, waving stiff ghost cuffs
of yourself from the rope as you left the house

to meet me in your end of town. Dulwich Pizza Hut.
Fondant-blue winter sun; warty gourds among
those laminate menus on the window-sill.
What does a girl in a wimple do when all that's left

of her knight is armour? The place was full of light
but there was shadow, too. Rings of black-purple
I didn't spot then but now remember,
bunched in there, waiting to spring.

## THE BURMESE *NAT* OF SHAPE-CHANGING AND BETEL-NUT SENDS A DREAM TO THE CORRUPT OFFICIAL WHO ORDERED THE BEHEADING OF HIS SECRET BELOVED

I am Mercury, huffing blue air; the Anahuath Jewel
    paraded by the Demoiselles of Xipe
who created the sun. I am the Mayan Long Count
    which will end on 23 December 2012;
an element it is not in your nature to know:

one of the wild ungulates of Yakutia,
    the night-tide of Gaviscon, clearing the route
for your Porkinson's Banger. I am the question you asked
    when I heard you were wretched and called in to help.
'Aren't you *dead*?' I was the steadiest dream

you ever had. At least, you thought so.
    I was the one you were faithful to, the prism edge
of mirrors you masturbated into thinking of me
    in Cuba, Sri Lanka, the South China Seas.
The waters of Zion you wept in, the *lacrimae rerum*

sparking your eyes at Sinatra's *one for his baby,*
    *one more for the road*. I kept you safe.
When the crisis fell at court, I got myself lost
    for your sake. I was true blue
but you sleight-of-handed me into the slippery bend,

the Bell's Scorpion on the path that had to be squashed.
    I know you did not mean to be what you are, feel bad
as you do. I know how you worry. I used to comfort you,
    soothing the *what-do-they-think-of-me*'s away
through gold coin of afternoon, silver currency of night,

till we'd see a hoopoe's crest bronze-pencilling the dawn
on shredding mist along the Irrawaddy, where ageing men
must exercise, by law. You'll be one of them soon.
I hear the *tonk tonk tonk* of a coppersmith bird
among the pyathats. In the palace, Lord White Elephant

receives his *petit déjeuner* of milk, from breasts
of a hundred young mothers. I see you manoeuvre
for merit, pay for gold-leaf on the dome of the new
Queen's pagoda. Biting your nails to the quick
(and the jagged skin around the sides), you attend

an audience with the Lion Throne. But what I think of you
where I'll be ever after: that's your achievement, too.
I won't call again. This is Only-Light-to-See-Veins-
in-the-Hand Time and I, on my spotted-winged
fruit bat, am off now. The end.

# THE PAZYRAK NOMAD

Cups. Hot water. We're going to thaw the permafrost
left by ghylls slapping down from the Altai Mountains,
slipping through nail-holes of her tomb
while our own world got made, to play the ice-masseur
on her tattoos – these crazed vermilion foals
whose fetlocks end in flames
as mazy as the copyright history of *In the Mood*.

Other women were sacrificed for men, with men.
She died herself alone. When we broke the roof
we found six horse skeletons cling-wrapped
in breaking goldfoil. Skin, full of tannin. Gut,
a lunette of glass. This halo of copper screw-studs
round her head means what was inside was special.
'Possibly,' Ozinsky says, 'a storyteller.'

Her optic nerve is severed, eyes gouged out,
sockets stuffed with Marsh Oxalis. Centuries melt
in an hour. Twenty thousand years since she saw sun
or it saw her. Someone, I hope her lover, left a fly-whisk
at her side. This plume of addled mane-hair, shot
with equine parasites, tells Ozinsky when she died –
second half of June. Funny last gift.

To flap away horse-flies in the Pazyrak underworld?
Memento of their last wild ride? Or just the only
thing he had to give, since she
was heading off before him – as she always did,
aflame in her copper tiara, coursing
her six untameable sorrels and greys
at the red horizon, and alone?

# THE SOHO LEOPARD

*for Patsy Rodenburg and Antonia Franceschi*

I was never your devoted lover. It was gossip,
   That. All wrong. I am the Amur leopard no
      One knows about, the thirty-fifth, each eye
An emerald. I'm passing by Quo
   Vadis, St Anne's Court and Sunset Strip

On a summer evening trembling – water-muscle
   Breaking on the knife-
      Edge of a dam – with promises of headlong
Encounters that might change a life.
   I never ended everything between us, so

You wouldn't lose your house and kids,
   Endanger school fees and the tax rebate,
      Your salary, your mother's Irish bonds.
That wasn't me. It was a question of identity,
   Mistaken. Poachers will get me anyway by and by,

So the mafia can re-package me
   As *os pantherii*, yellow pills in ivory hexagons
      Brush-painted with a Cinnamon Tree
Hieroglyph, the remedy
   For impotence in Hong Kong.

But I'm still leopard now: frostfur, quicksilver, planting pug-
   Marks all the way down Dean Street, past Café Lazeez,
      Trying not to hear through the open door
Of the Crown and Two Chairmen
   That ballad you used to sing, 'You Needed Me'.

I'm watching saffron awnings spill white zeds of light
   On Il Siciliano's pavement tablecloth.
      But catching my own reflection, rippling over
A Choi Sun figurine (the god of wealth, riding
   A tiger, holding a block of gold), in the window of

The Wen Tai Sun News Agency, gives me – or
   Let's take this out of self and call my leopard 'her' –
      A shock. She pauses, on the dimpled granite kerb
Of Chapone Place. She's all herself, and free,
   But this territory's patrolled

By her lost mate. She's wearing her endangered heart
   On every nerve-end, just in case
      His silvery silhouette and head-on-one-side smile
Pad up at the Webshack Internet Café.
   Dean Street? This is Dream Street. There's nothing here,

No one to marvel at the sole *nivalis* in the wild
   Zoologists still haven't counted.
      She'd send statistics reeling if they spied
Her rosette jigsaw of
   Black coral, broken daffodil.

★

She's considering gateways to another world.
   Stars of Orion's Belt, the Inca site
      Of ultimate creation,
Obsidian mines at Tuotihuacan
   Haunted by the gentle kinkajou,

The Pyramid of the Sun she climbed
   In the Avenue of the Dead,
      Bristling with the Storm God's hooky heads
And water-lilies streaming from his mouth,
   Or the cloisters of Quetzalpapalotl,

Palace-of-the-Quetzal-Bird-and-Butterfly,
   Guarded by parrot-gods with mica flames for eyes.
      She's got to send her leopard mind
Elsewhere. She really, really doesn't want to face
   What she's learning now about that mate of hers,

The centre of her jungle for five years. In a minute
  She'll have to stop believing he was good.
    Let her concentrate instead
On theatre lighting. Stage directions, say,
  For Beauty and the Beast.

                    ★

The palace is a star in the wrinkled forest
  And Beauty's got to go there of her own free will.
    She's afraid (she'd be mad not to be),
But she tells her dad, 'You mustn't doubt the Beast.'
  When she steps into Beast's kingdom

Avenues of paper pear-trees blossom
  And the audience hears tambourines. For this castle
    Is the world of melody, of sound. Every action in it,
Every thought, has its music counterpart. The clockwork
servants
  Brushing Beauty's hair are shimmery chromatic scales

On pipes and mandolin. Beauty warms her hands
  At the coal-scuttle's mystic grin,
    And we suddenly get guitars. Everything
Is lemonpale, invisibly policed.
  The carpet blushes peach for her delight.

Glass cases, caught in tinsel flakes of light from candelabra,
  Glitter with cup-hilt rapiers, schiavonas
    (Blades inlaid with jade and mother-of-pearl),
And a white-enamelled, silver-chased estoo.
  Beauty comes to rest on a crystal swing

That represents her heart. She's utterly at sea about what she's in
  For, who she's supposed to be, but she has ghost-faith
    In a Beast she's never seen. She can even hear him breathe.
'I'm aware you'll eat me, Beast,' she says into the wings.
  Judging by the noise, Beast must be ravenous.

His breathing is miked and amplified, the rasp
   Of Lord Darth Vadar from *Star Wars*. When Beast appears
      On stilts, a towering hedgehog-stork
In oriole feathers, whiskery chestnut fur,
   He has the face of a rubicund wart-hog

But you can see the actor's mouth behind the mask
   And living eyes – a sheepdog
      Listening for thunder – under diamond
Paste tears. When he smooths his fur wrist-ruffles
   (Beast is fond of money, and its fabrics) we can hear

Tchaikovsky strings in dominant sevenths:
   Sonic fireworks ripping to explosion
      In crashing north-east wind.
'All my rooms,' he says, 'are made
   To please you. All I want to do is give you joy.'

He may even think he means it. But, no getting away
   From it, she's a prisoner
      In his goldplate masquerade,
His Salon of Small Clowns in Millefiore Pink,
   His Hall of Singing Triangles and Mirrors.

★

That night she dreams she's dancing with a prince
   In snowy *crêpe de Chine*, a crimson turban, sash
      And scimitar. Next day
She finds a locket on the floor
   In the Chamber of Longed-For Harmonies:

A hum of cymbals when we glimpse
   The face within. That prince again, the one poor
      Beast is desperate to become.
Corridors echo with his whisper, 'Set me free.'
   The prisoner, you see, is Beast in the pelf and whirl

Of his own image, the enchanted-palace way
   He looks at things. But rescuing him will be a daunting task.
      What'll it take from you, girl? How if you give up your life
To save him from himself? What's real in him? Suppose
   He can only operate behind a mask

Or in a dream? Even princes are fiction,
   Mostly. What's the betting there's a man in there
      You'd turn out not to like? Too bad. Beauty has no
                                                    option.
That's the deal. Only someone who can treasure Beast,
   Trust him for what he is, can set him free.

★

Beauty, the stage directions have decided,
   Must be generous and strong. Devote
      Herself to his angry need, and long
For that wire breath on her throat at night. She's got to say
   With ninety-nine-carat genuine delight,

'My beloved is asleep all round me. This is who I am.
   I'm his.' She must feel welded to him,
      Welcome him in every orifice.
Any chamber he can find in her shall be his earth.
   She will protect him from

That sense he labours under that he has a skin too few,
   Instead of many. She must adore his Sinbad tongue
      Dancing sambas over hers, become a passionate
Prime-time fan of the prince within. Beast Beautiful,
   Beast Hero. Beast of the Platinum Sword.

19

She'll learn to calm his panic – at the giantess
   Behind these scenes, in dreams
      And in the sky: the mother-witch
Who turned him into Beast. Beauty'll cherish,
   And keep mum about it,

Beast-as-he-doesn't-wish-to-see-himself: as terrified.
   She knows the prince inside him won't survive
      Without her. She goes on,
However raw things get . . .
   What happened? There was rescue, yes,

But it didn't take. Maybe the witch-spell was too strong.
   Beauty escaped. She did it for his sake
      (He was torn in two, and holding him
Was trying to lullaby an earthquake),
   But also, if she's honest, for her own.

So this is the Amur leopard, the nearly-to-last
   On the hotline to your heart; calling
      From the Soho Theatre bar
To help you feel more easy with what' happened.
   You were my care. (I must have been your lover, after all.)

But the man you were with me was an endangered species
   And has left the world. Beauty slinks back
      To find her sweetheart sinking to the ground
In the Walk of Withered Roses. Treacherous, and blank
   About it. No more songs. And no other way to tell

This story, play this scene, apparently; though I,
   In every *alias* I can think of, hanker after one that's kinder
      To them both. The Beast (or Prince, whatever) falling
Back in her arms that always, always wished him well, to –
   What did you expect? To die.

# II

## THE KING'S CROSS FOXES

*For Richard Wentworth*

# THE TOTTERIDGE VIXEN

*January: Storm Moon*

Start of the mating season. Peak travel and dispersal time.
Fighting in silence, up on hind legs, ears flat

against flange of the head,
they are ice-shadows rampant,

snarly ghosts flowing, a snap and a vanish,
brushes bannering behind,

needling the rime along Carnoustie Drive,
clogged gutters of rainslicked kerb

on Stranraer Way. All for the new recruit
on Copenhagen Street: the teenage vixen,

banished from her mother's patch
in Totteridge Fields. Listen.

Her three-stanza bark, coughed scream
in the dark, that could be a murder, a child.

# EXCAVATION

*February: Chaste Moon*

Travelling ends. Fur's losing condition.
Each ginger hair-tip will snap. Rubbed patches appear
on the rump as they squeeze into underground tunnels,
flatten themselves under fences in wet sieve of rain,
scuff through concrete holes, four inches square.
Greeting the year with a clear soul, she looks
for a family earth. Her mother, her grandmothers, dug
in cement – under lock-ups, a doorstep, a grave;
this tower of Ford Capris in a breakers' yard.

Try these twigshadow brambles, back door of the Free
Metal disco, a narrow space in Argyle Walk above
a fourth-floor false ceiling; the architects' office.
Flub in through an air-brick and broken pane
to some under-the-kitchen haven in Brill Place.
Go on, sweetheart, look, all dry; and warmed
by the cladding and pipes. Room for the cubs to play . . .
No way. Fifty days pregnant, three to go, she's eeling
under a flatpack shed on Coopers Lane.

# TAKEAWAYS

*March: Seed Moon, Period of Becoming Aware*

She doesn't get out. Two weeks holed
up in here, curled round fur sausages, three
of them – black, deaf and blind – under the duvet
of her brush. Handlebar swirl of dark lines
down her pin-muzzle – up to listen, down to lick,

to stimulate circulation. She's a curled C
holding her top hindleg in the air for hours
not to squash the far cub. Forearm crooked like a sick
hound over the strongest, the first. One thin foxglove
tenderpaw over the lot. And he,

in silverdark frost and blue mists of King's Cross,
forages Timber Yard, Randell's Road,
Long Cedar Way, where night's tide has pasted
the ruck of rimmed gravel and mud
with condoms, beer cans, Lord

Cappuccino's wing-handle empties.
With his vomero-nasal organ (smell-cells
behind front teeth in the mouth's ribbed vault),
and two hundred million scent-receptors
(humans have five) packed in his nose –

so granulated, wet, and mad for pungency –
he digs detritus in a smellscape, brightening
all neural pathways to olfactory
arenas of his brain. He brings what he can.
Voluted Kentucky Fried Chicken bones,

maggoty pigeon's left wing. Fat brown slug,
a wet-glisten Havana cigar. Prawn Pot Noodle.
With a low whine, a whimper, he bows
his black mouth, leaves spice trade for her
at the lip of their ludo-cup earth.

# PLAYTIME

*April: Hare Moon, Period of Curiosity*

The cubs are unstoppable. Chivvy them back
and they flow to the light. They want to get on,

get a life. They emerge from the earth.
Choc brown at first, but here's good fox-ginger

flushing up round their cloud-navy eyes
while their parents start on the moult – feet

first; then rump, tail, shoulders; and head.
The corrugated, scruffpatch, moth-eaten look,

new coat flaming up under as old hair is shed.
Dogfox brings toys for the kids. Watch them chew –

throw – catch in mid-air. Spitting, galumphing;
as kittenglee, as rough and tearaway,

as spring hares dancing
on green hills these cubs'll never see.

From front lawns of Crofters Way,
or on the builders' mile

where Tunnel Link is Trojan
warhorse, pawing at sphinx-chippings,

scooping a platinum wasteland, a moonscape –
he'll scrump hamburger cartons, sharp-

crackle crisp packets, toy stegosauruses, playdough.
Watch it: you'll lose

whatever you leave out at night. A Flora Oil bottle,
perfect rattle, with a pebble, for any toddler fox.

An arm off a Barbie Doll. Knickers
from washing lines. Shoes.

# WORMS

*May: Dyad Moon, Period of Behavioural Refinement*

One cub has died on the road. Magpies
have eaten her. The last two play-learn, eat solid food
and follow their parents through dusk. Twins
of the Greek night sky, Castor and Pollux, shine
through damp London nights as earthworms
leave burrows. Parents spoon crane-flies off lawns
with their tongues, teach young to deadhead the bins

on Bemerton and Havelock, lift black plates
for frankincense, rot-lustre gems
of sunk baconfat. To strip flaking bark
for silverheave woodlice, listen
for worm-bristles rasping through grass.
If worm-tails are gripping the burrow –
even a worm can be frantic – the grey-black lips

pull gently taut – and pause – and pull again.
A technique used by bait-collecting fishermen.

# MOUSE LEAP

*June: Mead Moon, Period of Environmental Awareness*

They've left the breeding earth, open blue eyes
to new treasure, the light of late June.
Fieldmice should be running for organdie
hedgerows, green meadows scything for hay,

and it's time to try the Mouse Leap, that four-paws fly-
jump, high-jump, copyright of every vulpine fox.
First go, by Grand Union Canal. No –
yes! – look – curved in mid-air,

a flash-scarlet circumflex, three foot above
earth, bindweed, fag-ends: then dive,
front paws first, to counteract up-leap of vole.
One squeak of fire, and then still.

# THE WATCHERS

*July: Wort Moon, Herb Moon*

Under oilbarrels, boxes, nettles, the day retreat:
two cubs, lying up. The vixen has stopped giving milk.
In woodland they'd be watching herbs, and worts
(marjoram, wild spinach, chickweed), fall to the knife
to be dried under rafters, stored for winter infusions.
But these two this morning are quaffing the scent of a girl,
all denim trainers, eyebrow stud, nerves. She slinks
to the tow path, Camley Street Bridge, dips braids

in the jade-green canal, her chin upside-down
under scum of the sodden log edge, slicks hair
for her first fashion shoot. She thinks she's alone.
They're russeting up into amber and rose.
Blue eyes have turned citrus. Brown ears
(little triangles, no longer round) hear her ring-tune:
*Dr Zhivago*. She runs, disappears up the bridge.
They don't make a sound, but the catlike canine –

the small alfalfa flame, fisher of worms and beetles,
delicate predator whose fossils dot the Pleiocene
strata of North Africa, the forests of Indonesia
(oldest jungle in the world), is galloping the tow-path
(one falling in, to be drowned), checking run-holes
with new-grown *vibrissae* (stiff whiskers over the muzzle,
under chin, down back of forelegs.) Slipping safe
under wire in Rufford Street, Killick Street, Balfe.

# RED HARVEST

*August: Barley Moon*

He sleeps apart from parents now, or they do
from him. To get away – he's so demanding,
reckless-bright – she makes a precision leap
up a breezeblock wall in All Saints Street.

Little sharpshadow, balletic follower
of Enki, Sumerian god, Greek Protector
of the Vine, Spirit of Rain in old Japan,
avatar of rice god Indari,

Sioux trickster, shape-shifter: all this is here
mate, beside you, or even above.
Sunbathing, slowing her heart-rate
on your extension roof. A marigold angel,

tight as a shoe-lace under her brush.
She has done what she came for,
now sleeps in her harvest
of rowanberry, cinnamon, rust.

# IN THE OPEN

*September: Blood Moon, Wine Moon*

Grape–cluster. Sacrifice. Pigs killed for winter
provision. Adults and cubs
look the same now: sorrelflame, split
conker, goldfish, marmalade; a splinter
of sanguine chrysanthemum,
tangerine sparkler–head, lit.

You meet him, your late summer fox, as you turn
off the lights, zipping back from a night with your girl,
and watch St Pancras' pinnacles
stamp phosphorous ribbons on a glory sky
of wine–dark lily, dawnglow apricot.

Here he is, sniffing. Those scenting–cells
wind you exactly. No mange, and no moult.
Parade of white shirtfront. A flame, horizontal,
with ears (one back, and one forward);
gilt eyes under fox–frown. And not – till
you brake, stop the engine – afraid.

# THE LONER

*October: Snow Moon*

The family's breaking. This is dispersal.
Scorpio nights closing in. On Freeling Street,
the last surviving cub. Tall as his dad, but a stranger.

Of all cubs dispersing this autumn, half die.
Run over; tangled in netting; trapped between
palings. Infection, rat-poison, thrown stones.

Listen. Find darkblister blackberries
glinting in shadow; a tryst with a mouse.
Crunch apple-cores, hips of the dog rose.

Beachcomb the slime of canal, dark altars of compost
heaps, birdtables. Yes: study to ambush small birds.
Start a map of your own where the gleamcurve

of railway-line muscle is sheafing itself to the East.
Albert Wharf. Donegal Street. Church of St Paul.
Lean pickings of Somers Town.

# STRAIGHT LINES

*November: Oak Moon*

High-risk time. Cubs are adults now – and,
if they can, grab the kingdom of weakening
parents, ranges of foxes that died. Fighting begins.

Dispersing foxes travel in straight lines
ignoring all obstacles: burst sewage,
motorway, floods. Come spring,

a third of the lot will survive,
weathering deepfreeze of winter
like the Druids' greenheart tree

in a sailor's song. As a captive
he might get nine years.
On the streets, one or two; never three.

Challenging uncles and dad
he's a pointy-eared oilslick Achilles.
Bright warrior, who will not live long.

# TERRITORIAL

*December: Wolf Moon*

The night of the year; and the mating. Each fox
will defend his new patch. Most vocal now,
and most active. Hear it, the triple bark,
over and over: the banshee

of vixen. They fight in the dark,
face mortal wounds, for survival, sex,
foodscraps; and to be themselves,
rulers of 0.3 kilometres or less.

Who they are. What they're for.
Twyford Street. Contested strips
of shadow in Bingfield Park.
Black moss under Maiden Lane Bridge.

# III

# SEX, SCARS AND ALLIGATORS

*for Jo*

# ORPHEUS' IMAGINATION AS A SUBTERRANEAN CAR PARK

I wouldn't know myself in your mind now. I see me
flim and flutter there: Eurydice,
whose death was 'all her fault',

in something like Ikea car park's hypogeum
studded with concrete pillars,
oiled puddles (shivering to medal-ribbon

when four-wheel drives shake ramps to upper floors)
and thrumming harps abandoned in this vault:
broken trolleys, silver *lamé* in dark.

# THE JUNGLE GARDENS

That secret, whitening hush,
Those theatre loops and falls of Spanish Moss,
Neither Spanish nor a moss but huge blond Ondine swags
Of *tillandsia usneoides*
Over dripping Arthur Rackham live-oak trees.

Edward Avery McIlhenny, 'Mr Ned' (second son
Of Edmund), was the conservationist – and boy,
Was conservation needed. Plume hunters
Had slaughtered all, or nearly all, the Snowy Egrets here
For hats. Hide-hunters were killing off the gators.

Spring 1892, Ned built bird-holdings over a lagoon,
Netted seven egret babies, fed them, then released them
In the fall. Watched them wing – kites he'd made, without
Their string – across the Gulf of Mexico.
Sometimes, he said, you have to just trust instinct

And let go. Next spring the birds were back,
Slow-mo arrivals with their friends. Now hundreds,
Thousands take off from this shivering
Quicksilver, specking to white sky
For South America and winter, then return

To designer nesting-platforms.
Mr Ned laid out his tropical wilderness
Around just them. Drive through with a little map
And lose yourself – there're no one else –
In platinum mist and seventy-five-foot trees,

Sheeny lakes and sky-scraper camellias
Hiding deer, raccoon, black bear and cottonmouths.
All still. If you get out, to watch a heron land,
Mosquitoes with the bulk
Of Yorkshire terriers fizz in the car.

I go for Mr Ned, his chubby jaw, bow-tie, obsessions.
His face in the frontispiece exactly that
Of his great-grandson, the guy we met. I love to bits
The way his work is vindicated now by herpetologists
Whose books lurk under 'Reptiles'
In the Fellows' Library at London Zoo.
A pioneer! A reptile conservationist! Because,
Though amateur, he watched and knew –
Christ, *swam* with – them as a boy a hundred years ago,
In Bayou Chin and the small bayou that links Lake Cock
To North Vermilion Bay, between the cryptic
Tree roots, knuckles of horn and wood,
In copper-oilskin broken-crystal water
Whipped by a mugger's tail on goose hunts in the lugger.

He watched a twelve-foot female make her nest
Mashing a road through briars to lay her eggs.
He measured the uncoiling babies when they hatched.
(He had to tie her first.) Peeked from the nest-blind
Eight hours at a stretch as a bull hollowed out his den,
Tail wagging, carting mud away with tailscales, haunches,
Back and lower teeth throughout the night. Ned lived
Beside this reticent predator of the edge (evolved
For sixty-five million years) as we live now with cornershops.
I love the way he loved the ochre swivel of their eyes,
The high walk of an alligator – halfway between
A lizard sprawl and erect lope of dinosaur or mammal –
And left his papers (on the gators, on his birds)
To the State University in Baton Rouge.

# ON THE LAYOUT OF A VENTRICLE

... related more to birds, than lizards. For a start,
    They architect up their nests

From plants, lay calcified eggs in them, go in
    As dinosaurs must have done

For long-term parenting. Forget differing
    Molecular tissue of the skin:

Both birds and alligators boast an elongate ear canal,
    A muscled gizzard.

And in both, my friend, you find a total separation
    Of the ventricles of heart.

# BRIGHT CARPET, MIDNIGHT GLOW

The alligator's *tapetum lucidum* –
'Bright Carpet', the reflective layer
Behind the retina – is brimming with guanin
Crystals shimmering at night
Like they've taken fluorescent saffron to the lids.
An alligator eye is rimmed with yellow kohl
Smacking of a subterranean philosopher who knows
One day he'll do his reflective duty, see the light.
The eyes of adult males shine ginger-red.
Eyes of females and their young
Give off the greenish danger-glow
Of the witch-fire ball in Disney's *Sleeping Beauty*,
Hypnotising a princess to prick her finger.

Eyes, nostrils, ears, fit laterally on the head, high up
To breathe and detect their prey.
When the whole beast's submerged, the third eye-lid,
A transparent nictitating membrane, shuts
Like a visor. How an alligator protects itself
And its slowly metabolising brain: scute pairs, rigid
Ferrules wrinkled up on dorsal armour, spherical bony plates
Straddling segments of vertebrae in declining size.
We're looking at a living dinosaur
(From *deinos*, cognate with 'daemonic dread
And power'), oldest life-form on the planet!
Not that much evolution since the Late Triassic. Behold
Our window on the world of ruling reptiles, and their eyes!

# THE FEATHER OF TRUTH

There's Sobek, croc god of Lower Nile,
   Holding his *ankh*, symbol of eternity,
In one right paw or webby foot (whatever
   – His dappled, fingery front-flipper),
And sporting this Feather on his upright back
At forty-five degrees. A Truth to shake,
As you flash dreams, to All-Seeing Helios, or Sun.

No crocodile tears for him. Under the amber eye of Sobek
Failure to speak the truth, my lad, is death.

Alone and dormant in a self-dug den
   As dark as that twelfth candle at the wake
Your ancestors kept unlit for Judas
   (Who no doubt came, as you'll come too,
On Sobek in his dreams), deprived of sight
When the burrow's sussurant micro-climate
Dims, gators fall to tonic trance and cannot move.

# VERSIONS OF ALLIGATOR CREATION

She made the world's first alligator from a spine
Of sugar-cane,

Binding the spring growth's joints and knuckles,
Then rind-peelings,

The eyes from saffron, tail from leaves and fruit
Of betel-nut,

Clay mould from a sheet of upish
Squelching from sheaths

Of betel-nut palm: and prayed
It might have life.

Along the Yellow River, China's Sorrow,
The lemon-eyed

Chinese alligators burrow. Brandishing their mouths
Of burning torches,

Their breath of brindled coals, and guided by their Lord,
The Long Dragon,

They foretell rain in the Celestial Empire
With their calls.

## INSIDE THE ALLIGATOR'S MOUTH IS PART OF ITS OUTSIDE BODY

Pity the Louisiana alligator, that flashy, sequestered hide,
That inability to understand someone else's mind
Or any of the more evolved life-forms, except as prey.
His vulnerability. His wishing to do better
That somehow never surfaces for long. A greedy child
Whose mouth's inner skin belongs to his outside surface,
Sealed by a cartilaginous flap from the hungry throat.
Unlike the Tomistoma or false gharial (they attack

Unprovoked), he has no salt glands stippling his tongue
And can be timid. But everyone sees him as a primitive.
The unpredictable; the predator who flows with ambery, light-
Reflecting tears and then strikes back, in passion.
As if, setting out to oil-charm with a smile,
He first of all sealed his soul in boiling saffron.

# THE ALLIGATOR'S GREAT NEED AND GREAT DESIRE

To be thermally, forever, stable. (That surprised you.) Harder
                                        than it seems,
But thermo-regulation is their thing. When the air
    Is colder than the water, October to late March,
        They keep to dens below the water table.
            Away from them, caught by a cold snap, they become
Completely numb, incapable of moving. All they do is breathe
    Surface-oxygen through air-holes. Temperature is their goal,
Their god and good. During winter they take no food.

They pick an under-hang of lake or stream which will
    Stay filled with water when the spring freshet recedes.
        Listen to Mr Ned. 'See him,' he says, 'back out of that hole
            He's making, burdened with dollops of soft mud
                In his mouth and on his tail, pushing a mass of mud
With webbed hind feet. He's one busy alligator, sweeping his
                                                    tail
    From side to side. And trees round gator holes grow
Darker green, their roots enriched by droppings.'

For water's everything. The darkest alligators come, thought
                                        Ned,
    From Tupelo Gum Swamp where the flow is black,
        Dyed by its maker's hand – the bark, roots, fallen leaves
            Of Tupelo Gum. Gator holes, especially of older beasts
            Who, weary, cannot want to move,
Run a long way underground. That's how they manage. They
                                                    survive,
    When they can't bear what's outside. They know, whatever
                                                knowing is
For them, they'll have to face the winter. So, they dig.

# HEAD SLAP AND WATER DANCE

Courtship begins any time in April.
Takes a month. They leave the dusky-ducks,
The musk-rats, rails and ibis, yellow-crowned
Night heron, more or less alone. The female

Nuzzles at his snout and head (enriched
With sensory receptors);
Glands on mouth and cloaca secrete
An oily musk: attar of alligator,

Green silk slipping on the water
Marbled sheen at nostril level.
There's a lot of bellowing
Together (well, you've got to, haven't you?)

And throwing up of harmonising throats.
The one soft spot, the only place you hurt.
Another signal of flirtation, in the male,
Is slapping your head on water

Whilst snapping those jaws shut
And flailing your glorious rude tail
Making alligator angels, luminous parasols
Of up-then-down mosquito-breeding rain.

This is the high point of male display.
The order, in the diagram, is this.
One: alligator inhales, and swells a bit.
Two: the head is lowered.

Three: the head is tilted and the tail is arched.
Four: he rumbles with sub-audible vibrations
And white-tissue water on his back
Begins to dance.

Five: he gives a bellow, start
Of the head–slap–jaw–clap stuff, elevates
His head and body (head oblique,
Tail wagging), yawns his jaws apart,

Then whacks his head on the rolling boil
Of the water–surface, clapping his jaws bang shut
In the same millisecond, leaving crumpled scum
Through all the bayou, stiff as beaten cream.

Sex happens in the water. If she cruises deeper
He swims after. If she crawls on land
He'll follow. As she lies in the shallows, he
Will dock beside her like a gondola

And with his left forelimb begin to stroke
Her dorso–lateral region
Above the hedonic dorso–lateral gland, i.e.
Her rump. Gator love: first base

In a sunbather's seduction. Finally
He confronts her, puts his head –
Jesus, that head, it's most of what he's got –
Beneath her own, butt-rubs her throat

With bony plated segments of his skull,
Blowing great streams of bubbles past her cheeks,
Then slides his body over hers, twining
Her horny length,

Folding her in stubby forearms
Till the bases of their tails are interlaced.
That does it. All those boiling-jelly
Bubbles hit the spot; she lets him in.

# THE BUDDHA OF THE BAYOU

She'd have liked to see an alligator senate
Gather on the white-marsh bank,
Heads up, beaks wide apart to let
Water-lice around their teeth dry out.

But nothing. She didn't know where they were
Or where she was. Leafless azaleas, dripping mist,
A flappy coloured map, a gearless car
Buzzing with mosquitoes; pools, glades, dew-hush

Over duckweed's hummingbird skin.
One distant purple heron, a Dinka spear-master,
Fishing. The place flowed round her like his hands.
She's in a Chinese garden, climbing steps cut

Through a cup of seven hills
Above a cat's-eye lake. On top, A glass pavilion:
Columns carved as gilded bamboo parasols
Over a twenty-five-foot Buddha.

A spore-spotted
Sunrise Boddhisattva, keeping watch
Through two-thirds-slitted eyes
On black-marble greenweed closing on a trail

Furrowed through by submerged animal.
You can push your fingers up
Above the pedestal, even hold a palm
Against the Buddha's thigh.

# DOWNLOADING GOLDEN BUDDHA

Bingo! Gifted to the McIlhennys, 1937,
Tenth-century moonglow hardwood

From the Place of Rest in Thailand,
Home of titanic Buddha silhouettes

Against the Festival of Lights.
He has survived ten centuries,

Marauders, horsemen, trailer parks,
Plus the mad long journey here.

His upper torso's on your Sony laptop.
If you highlight him, the lips

Are frosted violet
Lipstick for Halloween

And his half-closed eyes
(Squinnying down across that jade

Jacuzzi for the McIlhenny gators)
Light suddenly within.

'Be still,' says the highlit Buddha
From deeps of your six-inch screen.

The azaleas and bamboo behind him
Now are night. 'Be still. Be very still.'

# THE ALLIGATORS DELIVER AN UNDERWATER ANTHEM ON HUMAN WOUNDS

'Listen to the beautiful deeds of which your cells are capable,
Though our cousin the salamander's cleverer than you,
Can lose a limb and grow a new one, skeleton and all.
Mammals have few tissues that regenerate.

Your severed muscles don't grow back.
Even your hair-roots are too complex to re-make.
(There's something to be said for primitive.)
You heal by patching up the epidermis, make good loss

Not with original cells but material that's handy, cheap
To fabricate, and simple (biologically) as a shoe.
Connective tissue, tough and soft – a kind of cobbled suede –
Consists of fibres (elastin, collagen,

Or mucopolysaccharides) in a jelly infill.
Scattered through this self-made jungle
Are the fibroblasts: the cells
Who build it now and dwell in it.

Think what a wound creates. Anarchy of spilling blood,
Bacteria, dead cells, foreign matter (rust, maybe,
Or chemicals). How does your body cope?
With tricksome mopping that you know

As inflammation. Blood-flow around the injured area
Increases, white blood cells rush in
With antibacterial proteins, and the injury itself
Triggers mechanisms for its cleaning up.

*Healing by first intention*, when bacteria don't interfere;
*Suppuration*, when they do. Both methods get the same result.
Plug holes with granulation, covered by
Black burgundy. The scab. How you heal.

Granulation closes margins of the wound, contracting tissue
Like jaws of soldier ants. The tickling you feel
Is from this shrinking star. You end with a bumpy mass
Of fibre with few living cells. The scar.'

## OPEN SECRET

This Buddha knows the history of wounds
and medical definition of a scar,

and doesn't think much of either.
If he dished out advice

(but he doesn't does he, he's a Buddha),
he would say,

'Repeat this mantra
on your prayer-wheel every day

before the yak-fat lamp.
"I won't put up with dead cells in my tissue

thanks. Too bad, if my wounds ache.
I may be burnt ground now

but burnt will grow back green
as nutria in the Atchafalaya Swamp."'

# THE WISHING STONE

*In front of many images of Buddha and of* nats *(indigenous spirits), you
will see egg-shaped stones about 25 cm diameter. We pray, 'If my wish
will be granted, may this stone be light as a feather', and lift the stone.*

*Guide to the Shwedagon Pagoda*, Yangon

Everyone lives by stories. These were ours.
The lies

We twist like dough, watch rise,
And feed ourselves

To make a past and future we can bear,
Are also story-shaped. Stories

Are what we face the mirror with.
This was the last we shared.

# IV

# NIGHTS OF THE DRY MONSOON

# THE WIND OF A THOUSAND YEARS

Spring, and a thunder moves mountains and rivers.
In moonlight, grass blows wildly; trees are whipped in two.

Tiger is invisible force. A great wind searches, blows
for a thousand years. Only by distant signs

will you know a tiger is here. Watch the moon
in a high night sky, hear crags in the forest shiver

when he whistles and booms. Down centuries
the tiger has walked, head down

with a click of the spine, through our dreams.
What fame he has won in our country!

Only demons can stand in his presence.
In foothills of mountain, the roar

raises rustle and rush in the valley, wakes tallest oak,
cork tree and pine. Tears open the sky.

# HE CLEARS HIS HEART IN CLOUDS

Lord of deep hidden places, where the goral
are silent. Spirit of ancient warriors, heroes' deeds.

Setting sun throws his terrible shadow: the world awaits
its master. At snap of a twig

other animals vanish. High wind swoops
through long grass. His presence is shadow in forest;

all tremble beneath. Unmatched in will and violence
he clears his heart in clouds, and he springs.

## TIGER'S BLESSING

Tiger's roar and dragon's murmur.
Favourable winds, they say. A perfect climate.
Mountains answer valleys, echoing the roar.
People prosper, the realm grows strong.

# CREATING THE TIGER

Before his skeleton and silhouette
defined all epiphanies
which Nature was intending,
from her goodness, to give,

Nature hesitated, shy.
Small girl alone, untried – new sash,
bruised feet – before her great event.

Then Nature loosed the hyoid bone
vibration in tiger's throat.
That voice
re-ordered the course of the world.

His tar-flare gaze
took in rivers, high forest,
scribbled pinnacles of rock.

# HERMIT

Deep mountains enclose my retreat.
Many men fear tigers. I
love to live in mountain,
where you see

many signs of a tiger,
scrapes in black earth
or arrogant claw-scratches high
on white birch; but few signs of men.

# THE FORESTS ARE FALLING

There is no bamboo in the forest any more.
The king of the mountain is migrating to the plain.

Without beasts, without trees,
what can the birds do?

The grass is black on Xang Po hill.
Even the dragon in water is threatened.

# THE PAINTER AND THE GENERAL

*A zoo in Nanchang, capital of Jiangxi province, has shackled a tiger to a table, charging sixty dollars to have a photo taken sitting on its back.*

China News Service, April 29th, 1996

In his *Hermitage of Redoubled Clarity*
Li-Quu-Dahu
paints tigers with a taste for eating men,
but I say men are worse than any tiger.

They call the General 'Tiger'.
He rides into town
down the Street of the Dragon's Tail,
green jade on his bridle clicking

in time with his sword.
But for a real tiger, vanquishing
enemies is the day's work.
Not extraordinary at all.

# THE FOREST, THE CORRUPT OFFICIAL AND A BOWL OF PENIS SOUP

How can I paint *Winter Landscape with Temples
and Travellers*, or *Five-Colour Parakeet*

*on Blossoming Apricot Tree?*
The oracle boxes are empty

and the Minister with a Brief for Charming Explanation
has signed a licence (to the army) for the forest to be cut,

ordered satin linings to his red kimono
and is drinking with the General

in what he says is the best restaurant in town,
attended by two fifteen-year-old girls:

handpicked, translucent brown jade.
Black tree stumps cool on the mountain,

sawmills slide out planks a hundred an hour
and white ash blooms over the river

while the courtier treats the General
to tiger-penis soup, five hundred *linu* a bowl.

I'll paint the bare burnt mamillated plain,
Flame of the Forest in its white and scarlet,

jack fruits and jacaranda, the stag in the sky
and the naming of stars, the three definitions of twilight

in Yunnan province where white-handed gibbons
used to sing their love duets.

I'll paint the truth of illusion, a glossary
of atmospheric optics,

and Guanyin, Guardian of Compassion.
I'll pay particular attention to her smile.

# A QUESTION

Like rising wind and scudding clouds
snow-rolling over deep mountains,

the drunk painter is creating a shape.
Is that a tiger in the ravine,

or swirl of spiderline grain
in the rock? Let General Liguang answer.

# TIGER IS GRANDEUR OF NATURE

*Outside DJ Disco on Huafa Road, Shenshen, a neon sign says 'Dance with the Tiger'. Inside, strobe lights and music swirl through Deng Deng's revolving cage. 'It is not dangerous,' said marketing manager Liu Yong. 'We have pulled out her claws and teeth.'*

*South China Morning Post*, May 13th, 1996

Above his eyes, whose iris is the umber
of the general's uniform when wet,
the Venerable Tiger
bears upon his brow the hieroglyph for King.

Seeking food in tiger's mouth is to engage
in hazardous occupation. To be saved
from tiger's mouth is wonderful escape.
You catch lice on tiger's head? You are daring boy.

His name means Sovereign, Whetted, Brave.
His element is metal. (Gold is needed, to rule men.)
When a tiger dies, his soul sinks into earth
and will return as amber.

## SUNDOWN

I will make my hermitage here
on this emerald-feather mountain
where a tiger drives people away.
On nights of the dry monsoon
his long roar blows through the valley.

Evening wind, and the young river
fresh from its source ripples white
lace waves, stirs reeds on the bank.
Setting sun is a syrup of goldsilt, suspended
in cashmere-swirl, brown-olive mud.

Under a late-rising moon the tiger comes.
Black dancing grass-heads, rose-purple cream
in the daylight, are holding their breath.
No merely wealthy life is worth living.

# SIGHTING THE TIGER

Shitao is famous for pencil-line detail,
for textures. Jianjiang can paint

the inner structure of a mountain.
Both spent half their lives

on Huang Mountain, but never caught a flash,
not a molecule, of the divine – that patchwork glow

of a hiding tiger, sizing you up from the shadow
of lemonberry, spiny bamboo.

Working outward
from the self through animals to

the world, you hope to see new truths.
Scaling mountains

where there was no level rock or earth to rest,
pushing through forests thick in thorn

and pulsing undergrowth
where the white-lipped pit viper

curls and sags
on springing leaves –

just the height you might grab to steady you
in a steep, unknowing place –

I sought to paint
the spirit and will of the tiger.

## MARY'S ELEPHANT, ELIZABETH'S SPINET

In the British Galleries of the Victoria and Albert Museum, London, is a panelled linen hanging embroidered in tent stitch. Mary Queen of Scots, with the help of Elizabeth Talbot, Countess of Shrewsbury (Bess of Hardwick) and ladies of her household, created these panels during her nineteen-year imprisonment. (Queen Elizabeth put Mary in the custody of the Earl of Shrewsbury; she was held captive in various English country houses until she was executed.) The lowest panel is an elephant copied from C. Gesner's *Icones Animalium*. Mary combined her own emblem, the marigold turning towards the sun, with other emblems representing courage in adversity.

Right next to the hanging is a spinet: a small harpsichord with oblique strings. It is called a virginals when enclosed, like this one, in a box without legs. Its black keyboard has pale sharps and flats; the case is decorated with Elizabeth's arms and a device belonging to her mother Anne Boleyn: a falcon holding a sceptre. The whole thing is known as 'Queen Elizabeth's Virginals' and was probably designed for her by the Venetian instrument-maker Benedictus Florianus. Elizabeth was said to play 'excellently well when she was solitary, to shun melancholy'. Both cousins turned to art when they were sad.

To hold on to her own sceptre, Elizabeth had Mary executed in 1587.

*Unbroken forest*
By the time of the Domesday Book only twenty per cent of England was still under forest; after 1500 a lot of that was cut down, but there were still long swathes of forest between Elizabeth and Mary.

*Wolf*
Britain's last wolf was probably shot in Scotland in the 1740s.

This poem begins with something Socrates says to Alcibiades in a dialogue attributed to Plato, *Alcibiades I*. I first met it in a poem by George Seferis, '*Mythistorema 4*', which quotes Socrates as saying, 'If the soul is to know itself, it must look into a soul.' Seferis adds, 'The stranger and the enemy, we've seen him in the mirror'. He later said the Plato passage reminded him of Baudelaire's 'La mort des amants':

> Nos deux coeurs seront deux vastes flambeaux,
> Qui réflechiront leurs doubles lumières
> Dans nos deux esprits, ces miroirs jumeaux.

Alcibiades, a glamorous and charismatic patrician politician-soldier, joined Socrates' group of student philosophers for a while, and was later exiled because people suspected him of a sacrilegious prank in which all the herms in Athens (the guardian statues of Hermes) had their erect penises chipped off in a single night. It was a terrible omen for his own military expedition against Sicily the next day, which turned out disastrously and precipitated Athens' defeat in the Peloponnesian war. Socrates was later put to death partly because of his association with Alcibiades.

In one dialogue, the *Symposium*, Plato makes Alcibiades say he tried and failed to seduce Socrates. In *Alcibiades I*, when Alcibiades is on the point of going into politics, the subject under discussion is the nature of love. Alcibiades is courted by all; the hot question (what every politician also wants to know) is who really loves Alcibiades. Plato makes Socrates argue that he is the only one who really feels love for Alcibiades, because he loves his soul. Everyone else loves his body.

Citing the Delphic maxim, 'Know thyself', Plato's Socrates compares the image of itself which one human eye can see in another, with the idea that a human soul can only know itself by looking into another soul. This, Plato implies, is true love: when one soul sees itself reflected in another.

## YELLOW GOURDS WITH JAGUAR IN DULWICH PIZZA HUT

*Brothers-Would-Not-Know-Each-Other Time*
Twilight. These phrases for different times of day come from
F. Tennyson Jesse's 1929 novel *The Lacquer Lady*, set in the
court of the kings of Upper Burma, before it was invaded by the
British in the 1880s for the teak forests. Another such phrase is
used in the next poem.


## THE BURMESE *NAT* OF SHAPE-CHANGING AND BETEL-NUT SENDS A DREAM TO THE CORRUPT OFFICIAL WHO ORDERED THE BEHEADING OF HIS SECRET BELOVED

When Buddhism arrived in Burma, now Myanmar, it fused
with the indigenous religion: *nats*, spirits of place, especially of
forest. *Nats* have human form and ride on animals. In 2001,
while in Myanmar to do readings and workshops with local
poets for the British Council, I saw shrines to *nats* in Buddhist
pagodas, and also in trees, in countryside and town. Like saints
in the Catholic Church, *nats* act as personal intercessors and
intermediaries.


## THE PAZYRAK NOMAD

This poem started from a late-night TV programme on the
exhuming of an ancient woman's body in Siberia.

# THE SOHO LEOPARD

The Amur or Far Eastern leopard is a sub-species inhabiting the Russian Far East, south of Vladivostock, where Russia squeezes between China and the Sea of Japan. Only thirty are now known to exist in the wild. It was said to be thirty-four, when I wrote the poem.

Leopards as well as tigers are being poached all over Asia for their bones, which are ground up and used in Traditional Chinese Medicine.

*Quo Vadis, Sunset Strip, Café Lazeez, Crown and Two Chairmen, Il Siciliano, Wen Tai Sun News Agency*
Establishments in Dean Street, Soho, London, on the edge of Chinatown.

*St Anne's Court, Chapone Place*
Side streets off Dean Street.

*Tuotihuacan*
In the far northeast of the Valley of Mexico.

*Avenue of the Dead, Quetzalpapalotl*
In the complex of buildings around the Pyramids of the Sun and Moon outside Mexico City.

*schiavona, estoo*
Ancient swords or daggers.

*Salon of Small Clowns, Hall of Singing Triangles*
This poem began while I was watching a production of *Beauty and the Beast* at the Young Vic in which Beast created magical rooms for his reluctant guest.

# THE KING'S CROSS FOXES

It is now easier in Britain to see a fox in the city than the country. Foxes have moved into cities here more than any other country in the world, because we like fences round our gardens and foxes like the tangle they make.

Since urban foxes are a secret little flick of country in the town, I linked the rhythm of their life with ancient British names for the year's twelve full moons, named for seasonal human activities in the country.

## TAKEAWAYS

Noses of most vertebrates contain two sensory channels: the olfactory system and the vomero-nasal complex, a system that has its own separate organs, nerves and connecting structures in the brain, and detects pheromones. Our number of sense receptors is a fraction of what foxes possess, and the olfactory region of our brain is minuscule in comparison with theirs.

## MOUSE LEAP

Term for the move an adult red fox makes when it jumps in the air and comes down on small quick prey.

*Vulpine Fox*
There are three separate lineages of foxlike canids. The two gray foxes of North America belong to genus Urocyon; the eight species of zorro in South America to genus Dusicyon; and the twelve vulpine foxes of Europe, Africa, Asia and America, including Britain's red fox, to genus Vulpes.

## SEX, SCARS AND ALLIGATORS

This sequence was written in response to a paper called 'Scars, Sex and Alligators, Unexpected Discoveries in Bio-Medical Research' by Professor Mark Fergusson of Manchester University. While doing research on alligator embryos he found that their wounds healed without scarring.

## THE JUNGLE GARDENS

About 140 miles west of New Orleans a salt dome called Avery Island rises out of the Louisiana Gulf. Edmund McIlhenny began to make Tabasco sauce there in 1868; the McIlhenny Company runs the Tabasco factory there today. Edward Avery McIlhenny, Mr Ned, began his Jungle Gardens in 1892.

## INSIDE THE ALLIGATOR'S MOUTH IS PART OF ITS OUTSIDE BODY

*Tomistoma*
A gharial is a very endangered crocodilian with a long, curiously slender snout. The Tomistoma ('sharp mouth'), the Malayan fish crocodile living in lakes, rivers and swamps in Indonesia and Malaysia, has a very similar snout. But other things about it, from genetics to fossil evidence, put it in a different taxonomic class, so it is currently, rather unfairly, called the 'false gharial'.

## THE BUDDHA OF THE BAYOU

In a Chinese garden inside E.A. McIlhenny's Jungle Gardens is a large gold Buddha presented to him in 1937.

## NIGHTS OF THE DRY MONSOON

From the earliest surviving Chinese paintings, it was common practice for the painter to add a poem to a painting: so part of the painting of a tiger is a poem about a tiger. The Chinese have revered and painted tigers for over a thousand years.


## HE CLEARS HIS HEART IN CLOUDS

*Goral*
An Asian goat-antelope species of the Caprinae family. Tiger prey.